GHOSTS OF THE NILE

Words and pictures by Cheryl Harness

Simon & Schuster Books for Young Readers
New York London Toronto Sydney

Zachary, when the temples of Athens were new, and when young Alexander the Great was conquering the world, Egypt was already old. When Julius Caesar was leading the Roman armies into foreign lands, the pyramids had stood for 2,500 years and the sun of Egypt's power was setting. Oh, my dear boy, if only I could see Egypt as it once was! That would be my fondest wish come true.

Mom wanted us to take her spooky old aunt to the special Egypt of the Pharaohs exhibit at the museum. She'll fit right in—Great-Aunt Allie, I mean. She's pretty ancient herself.

ATLANTIC OCEAN
EUROPE
ROME
ATHENS
BLACK SEA
ASIA MINOR
CRETE
MEDITERRANEAN SEA
A F R I C A
EGYPT
NILE RIVER
ARABIA
RED SEA

She doesn't get out much, and you know, when I was little, she used to tell me all kinds of exciting stories about when she had gone there as a young lady.

To the museum?

No, smarty. To Egypt.

Okay. Great-Aunt Allie is one of those grown-ups who has to be a walking encyclopedia, and Egypt's her favorite subject. That's where she got her bug jewel, she told us.

Making Mud Bricks

TRUE PYRAMIDS

STEP PYRAMID

GIZA (AL JĪZAH)

SAQQARA MEMPHIS

DASHUR

BENT PYRAMID

NILE RIVER

Among the GHOSTS OF THE NILE?
No. You shall go back to the future
in a very little while.

KING DJOSER (aka ZOSER)
Father of the Pyramid

P E R I O D   OLD   KINGDOM

2ND DYNASTY 2857–2705 B.C.   3RD DYNASTY 2705–2630 B.C.

-TEP-SEKH-MWY   RENEB   NINETJER   SENED   PERIB-SEN   SEKH-EMIB   KHASEKH-EMWY   NEBKA I   DJOSER   SNEFRU   KHABA   HUN I

Ancient Egyptians believed that their bodies must be carefully preserved so that their spirits would have a home in the afterlife. Their preserved remains were placed in burial chambers in tombs made of mud bricks or stone. These bench-shaped tombs were called mastabas.

In about 2650 B.C. the brilliant doctor and architect Imhotep had the idea of stacking mastabas like a wedding cake of stone for the tomb of King Djoser (JO-zer). The chambers of the 200-foot-tall Step Pyramid held food, weapons, the records of Djoser's earthly glory, and so on: all he might need in the eternal afterlife. This forerunner of the true pyramid still looks like a stairway to heaven. It is the world's oldest stone monument.

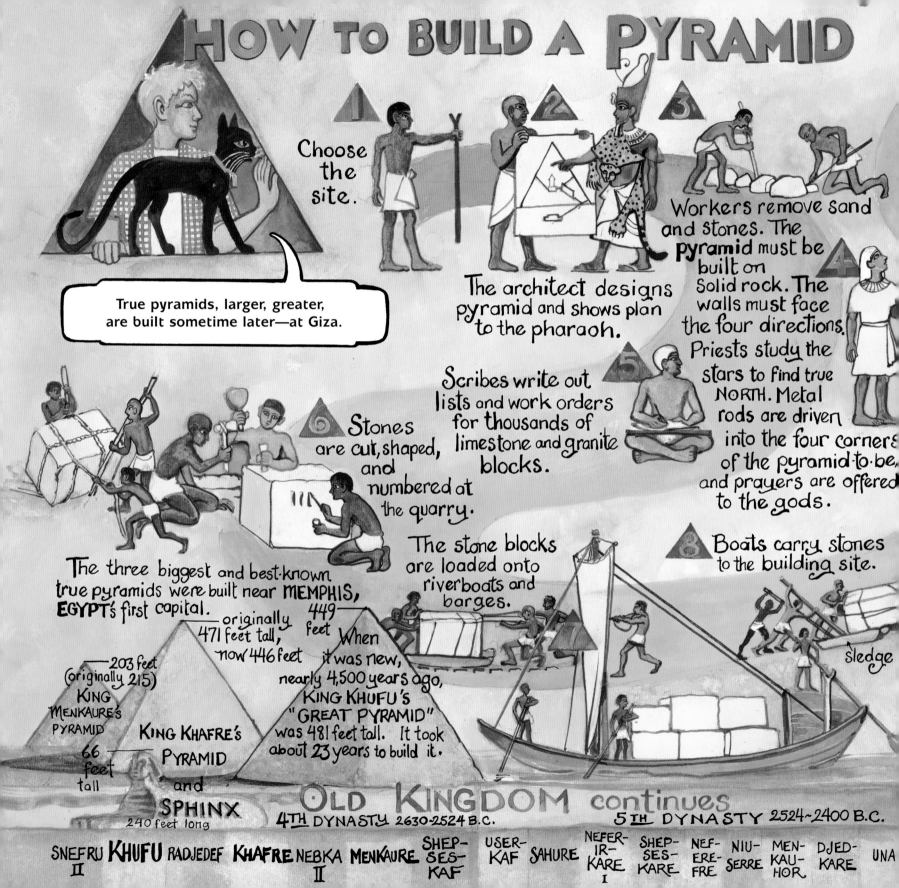

HOW TO BUILD A PYRAMID

Choose the site.

True pyramids, larger, greater, are built sometime later—at Giza.

1 The architect designs pyramid and shows plan to the pharaoh.

2 Workers remove sand and stones. The pyramid must be built on solid rock. The walls must face the four directions. Priests study the stars to find true NORTH. Metal rods are driven into the four corners of the pyramid-to-be, and prayers are offered to the gods.

3 Stones are cut, shaped, and numbered at the quarry.

6 Scribes write out lists and work orders for thousands of limestone and granite blocks.

5 The stone blocks are loaded onto riverboats and barges.

8 Boats carry stones to the building site.

The three biggest and best-known true pyramids were built near MEMPHIS, EGYPT's first capital.

203 feet (originally 215)
KING MENKAURE'S PYRAMID

66 feet tall

originally 471 feet tall, now 446 feet
KING KHAFRE'S PYRAMID

449 feet

and SPHINX
240 feet long

When it was new, nearly 4,500 years ago, KING KHUFU'S "GREAT PYRAMID" was 481 feet tall. It took about 23 years to build it.

sledge

OLD KINGDOM continues

4TH DYNASTY 2630-2524 B.C.   5TH DYNASTY 2524-2400 B.C.

SNEFRU II   KHUFU   RADJEDEF   KHAFRE   NEBKA II   MENKAURE   SHEP-SES-KAF   USER-KAF   SAHURE   NEFER-IR-KARE I   SHEP-SES-KARE   NEF-ERE-FRE   NIU-SERRE   MEN-KAU-HOR   DJED-KARE   UNA

The foundation must be level and true. Workers dig trenches around the site, fill them with water, and stretch lines parallel with the water's surface.

fill with stone

↑ cut away

TOOLS

SAW

CHISELS

MALLET

DRILL

HAMMER

The workmen's tools were made of wood, stone, and copper.

polishing stone

dolemite stone pounder

Using rope, wooden sledges, ramps, and rollers, gangs of workers haul, push, and drag stone blocks weighing up to 15 tons to the work site.

The foundation stones are carefully placed as underground passageways, slanting corridors, narrow air shafts, and burial chambers are made.

MORTAR

TROWEL

ADZE

As the first layers (courses) of stones are placed, RAMPS are built of

CAUSEWAY: covered passage between the valley temple at river's edge and the temple that will be built near the PYRAMID

rock and river mud. Using these RAMPS, workers build the tomb higher and higher.

The stones must be square, straight, and smooth.

BONING RODS

The string is pulled tightly and the third rod is slid along to show where the stone's surface is not even with the string. Rough stone is chiseled away.

PLUMB LINE: a tool used to find true VERTICAL

6TH DYNASTY 2400~2250 B.C.

7TH and 8TH DYNASTIES 2250-2213 B.C.

TETI   PEPI I   MERENRE I   PEPI II   MERENRE II   QUEEN NITOCRIS
lived to be 100 years old and history's longest-reigning monarch.

QAKARE   NEFERKAURE   NEFER-KAUHOR   NEFERIR-KARE II

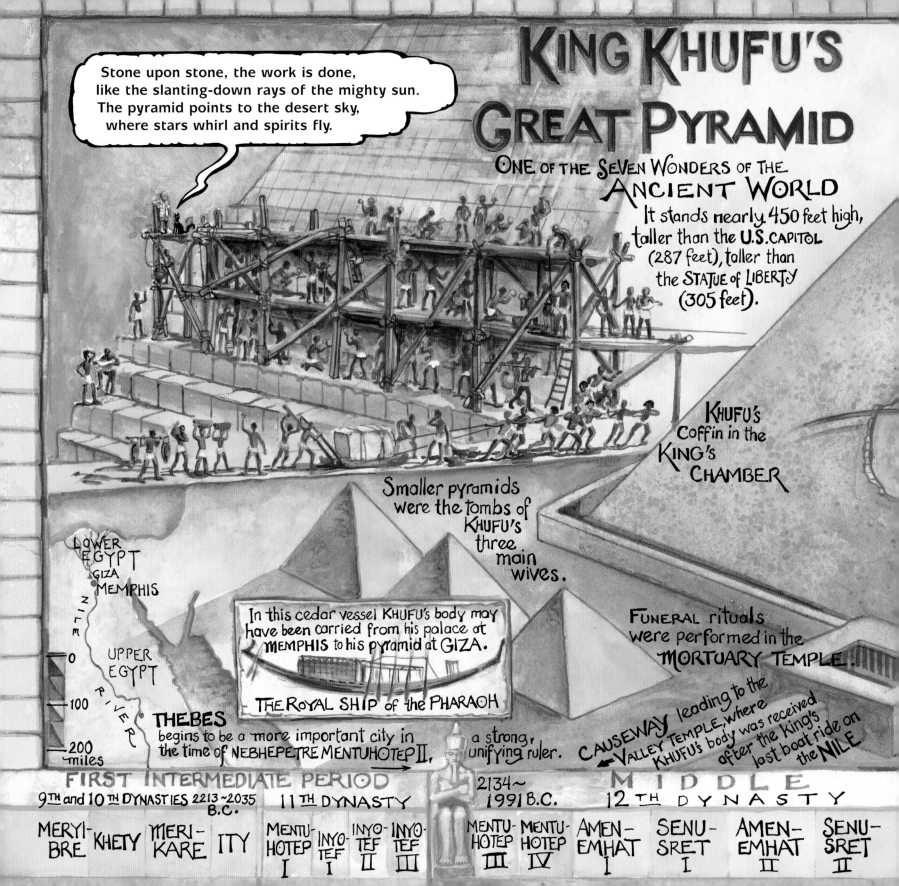

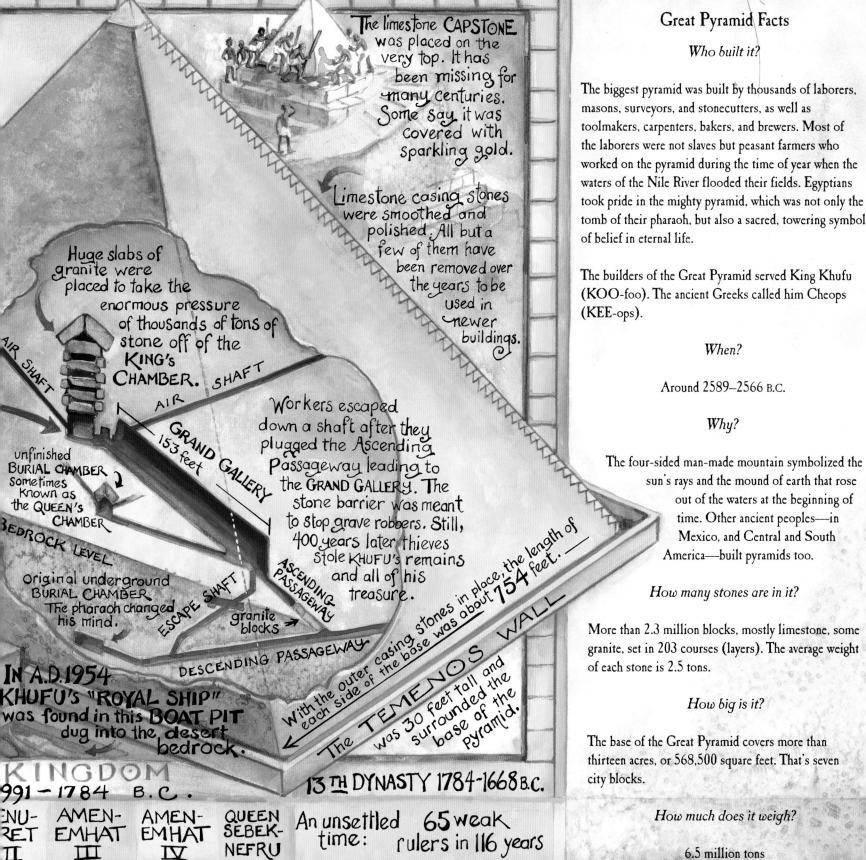

The limestone CAPSTONE was placed on the very top. It has been missing for many centuries. Some say it was covered with sparkling gold.

Limestone casing stones were smoothed and polished. All but a few of them have been removed over the years to be used in newer buildings.

Huge slabs of granite were placed to take the enormous pressure of thousands of tons of stone off of the KING'S CHAMBER.

AIR SHAFT

AIR SHAFT

AIR SHAFT

GRAND GALLERY 153 feet

Workers escaped down a shaft after they plugged the Ascending Passageway leading to the GRAND GALLERY. The stone barrier was meant to stop grave robbers. Still, 400 years later thieves stole KHUFU'S remains and all of his treasure.

unfinished BURIAL CHAMBER sometimes known as the QUEEN'S CHAMBER

BEDROCK LEVEL

original underground BURIAL CHAMBER. The pharaoh changed his mind.

ESCAPE SHAFT

ASCENDING PASSAGEWAY

granite blocks

DESCENDING PASSAGEWAY

With the outer casing stones in place, the length of each side of the base was about 754 feet.

THE TEMENOS WALL was 30 feet tall and surrounded the base of the Pyramid.

IN A.D. 1954 KHUFU'S "ROYAL SHIP" was found in this BOAT PIT dug into the desert bedrock.

KINGDOM
991 – 1784 B.C.

NU-RET II | AMEN-EMHAT III | AMEN-EMHAT IV | QUEEN SEBEK-NEFRU | An unsettled time: 65 weak rulers in 116 years

13TH DYNASTY 1784-1668 B.C.

Great Pyramid Facts

Who built it?

The biggest pyramid was built by thousands of laborers, masons, surveyors, and stonecutters, as well as toolmakers, carpenters, bakers, and brewers. Most of the laborers were not slaves but peasant farmers who worked on the pyramid during the time of year when the waters of the Nile River flooded their fields. Egyptians took pride in the mighty pyramid, which was not only the tomb of their pharaoh, but also a sacred, towering symbol of belief in eternal life.

The builders of the Great Pyramid served King Khufu (KOO-foo). The ancient Greeks called him Cheops (KEE-ops).

When?

Around 2589–2566 B.C.

Why?

The four-sided man-made mountain symbolized the sun's rays and the mound of earth that rose out of the waters at the beginning of time. Other ancient peoples—in Mexico, and Central and South America—built pyramids too.

How many stones are in it?

More than 2.3 million blocks, mostly limestone, some granite, set in 203 courses (layers). The average weight of each stone is 2.5 tons.

How big is it?

The base of the Great Pyramid covers more than thirteen acres, or 568,500 square feet. That's seven city blocks.

How much does it weigh?

6.5 million tons

Hold your breath—
look upon Death!

As always, folks wondered what would happen after they died. Surely their souls' journeys would go on and be as lively as life along the Nile—but what would the afterlife be like? Over thousands of years many answers to that question made up the rich, complicated religion of ancient Egypt.

Your soul had places to go, things to do. You'd need a just life and many prayers to face the judgment of Osiris, god of the underworld.

Your birdlike spirit might visit the living. Your soul might work in the heavenly Field of Reeds and go with the Sun God on his nightly boat ride through the Underworld. By day your soul might go back to the tomb for food, things you loved in life, and especially your body—your resting place. Your soul would always need to recognize its home. That meant that your body had to last and last throughout eternity.

The mummification rituals, prayers, and embalming could take as long as seventy days. The body was dried with a special salt, called natron, then carefully stuffed and wrapped with spices, tree resin, sawdust, and linen. The priests would preserve the person's skin with oils, and his or her soul with sacred charms such as the *wedjat* eye of the god Horus;

an ankh, which stood for the breath of life;

and a holy scarab beetle placed over the heart.

SECOND INTERMEDIATE PERIOD
14TH, 15TH, 16TH DYNASTIES 1720~1565 B.C.   17TH DYNASTY 1668~1570 B.C.

Eastern invaders, the HYKSOS, and their horse-drawn chariots come into EGYPT.

NEHESY

HYKSOS kings in Lower EGYPT

OTHER RULERS in THEBES in Upper EGYPT

AHMOSE I

Holy liquids and instruments were used in the ceremonial OPENING of the MOUTH, which permitted the SOUL to return into the body.

A priest wearing a mask of ANUBIS, the jackal-headed god of MUMMIFICATION, was in charge of the sacred business of turning a dead body into a MUMMY.

He looked out of the eyeholes.

The brain was pulled out through the nose with a special hook.

Then, with this funnel, RESIN would be injected into the nostrils to keep the skull from caving in.

A special knife made of flint was used to make the first cut.

The priests took out the body's innards, then preserved and placed them in four CANOPIC JARS topped with protector gods.

DUAMUTEF (jackal) QEBEHSENUEF (falcon) HAPY (baboon) IMSETY (human)

STOMACH INTESTINES LUNGS LIVER

The NEW KINGDOM will last 500 years.

18TH DYNASTY 1570 B.C. → EGYPT becomes the greatest power of the ancient world.

...rives the HYKSOS out of EGYPT.

AMENHOTEP I TUTHMOSIS I
The son and grandson of AHMOSE I conquer lands far beyond the valley of the NILE.

TUTHMOSIS II

NEW KINGDOM
MIDDLE KINGDOM
OLD KINGDOM

SYRIA
CYPRUS
LEBANON
PALESTINE
Mediterranean Sea
ARABIA
Red Sea
*THEBES CAPITAL of Egyptian empire
NILE RIVER

Egyptians created stories to explain their world, life, and death. The sun, the moon, and animals were woven into their religion of many **GODS and GODDESSES.**

People worshiped in the temples of the gods. They brought them food, flowers, and live or mummified animals as offerings.

(1) ISIS: the great goddess, protector of children
(2) OSIRIS: god of the underworld
(3) HORUS: falcon-headed god of light and heaven
(4) RE (aka RA): hawk-headed sun god
(5) ANUBIS: jackal-headed god of the dead and mummification
(6) NEPHTHYS: protector of women and of the dead
(7) BES: god of the happy home
(8) MAAT: goddess of truth and order
(9) SETH: donkey-headed god of chaos
(10) HATHOR: cow-horned mother goddess of love, music, and dance
(11) AMUN: god of Thebes
(12) SOBEK: crocodile god of fertility and water
(13) SHU: old creator god who parted (14) NUT, his sky-goddess daughter, from his earth-god son, Geb
(15) KHNUM: ram-headed Nile god
(16) PTAH: god of craftsmen; his symbol was Apis, a bull who was worshiped in Memphis.
(17) THOTH: ibis-headed god of wisdom and scribes
(18) BASTET: cat goddess and protector of mothers

AKHENATEN had changed his name. He tries to change EGYPT's official religion. He turns away from AMUN, the main god of THEBES. About 200 miles to the north he builds AKHETATEN, a new capital city dedicated to ATEN, god of the sun disk.

ALEXANDRIA

ROSETTA
The DELTA

AVARIS, HYKSOS
capital

GIZA
HELIOPOLIS
SAQQARA
MEMPHIS
DASHUR

OASIS
at
FAYUM

The god SOBEK's crocodile was kept at CROCODILOPOLIS.

The ibis of THOTH was kept at HERMOPOLIS.

Akhenaten's capital
AKHETATEN

THE RIVER NILE

Ancient EGYPTIANS made pilgrimages to the TEMPLE of OSIRIS at ABYDOS.

Many a NEW KINGDOM ruler, such as HATSHEPSUT and TUTANKHAMUN, were buried in the VALLEYS of KINGS and QUEENS across the NILE from THEBES.

TEMPLE of HORUS

TEMPLE of RAMSES II

TEMPLE of ISIS

TEMPLE of HATHOR
DENDERA
KARNAK
LUXOR
THEBES
EDFU

0 25 50 75 100 125
MILES

Obelisks, sphinxes, and temples, sacred to mighty AMUN, were erected at THEBES.

ISLAND of ELEPHANTINE
KOM OMBO

PHILAE ISLAND
ABU SIMBEL
ASWĀN
FIRST CATARACT (river rapids)

SECOND CATARACT

Modern EGYPTIANS built a dam at ASWĀN in the 1960s. It stopped the annual flooding of the NILE. The power of the river is used to make electricity.

BUHEN

THIRD CATARACT

A vast lake, LAKE NASSER, was formed by the modern ASWĀN HIGH DAM. The mighty temple at ABU SIMBEL had to be moved to higher ground or the four huge images of RAMSES II would have been lost under the waters forever. It was a great feat.

FOURTH CATARACT

Every year the Nile River swelled with all of the rains that fell upstream, to the south, in Ethiopia. As it flowed northward to the Mediterranean Sea, it spilled over the banks and flooded the land along the river. When the waters pulled back, they left behind rich black land: good for growing wheat, papyrus, barley, dates, flax for linen, and clover for goats and cattle. Along the long green riverbank oasis hippos, herons, crocodiles, and the civilization of Egypt flourished, the gifts of the Nile, longest river in the world. The Nile had six cataracts total, four of which are depicted here.

The 19TH DYNASTY comes to an end 1185 B.C.

RAMSES II

dies in 1213 B.C. after 67 years on the throne of EGYPT. He and his queen NEFERTARI and his other wives have nearly 150 children. His workers built many monuments and his warriors fought many battles for RAMSES the GREAT.

MERNEPTAH | AMENMESSE | SETI II | SIPTAH | QUEEN TAWOSRET

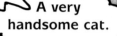

But what does any of that matter? We're here! On the old River Nile in Egypt's glory days!

Life on the Lively NILE

(1) Cargo ships carried all sorts of goods to river ports up and down the Nile.

(2) The farmer is using a shadoof to dip water from the Nile. The heavy weight on the end of the pole will pull up the bucket. He will empty it into his irrigation ditch to water his crops.

(3) This pleasure boat is made of wood.

(4) The Egyptians' earliest boats were made out of bound-together bundles of papyrus reeds. Ancient Egyptians may have sailed papyrus boats across the Atlantic Ocean to the Americas. The earliest sailboats were probably made by the ancient Egyptians.

(5) The huge, dangerous hippopotamus had no trouble at all overturning the Egyptians' boats.

(6) Detailed models of the boats and barges of noble Egyptians have been found in their tombs.

(7) Some present-day Egyptians still navigate the Nile in their swift, shallow feluccas (fuh-LOO-kuhs).

(8) Nile crocodiles could grow as long as twenty-two feet.

NTERMEDIATE PERIOD

DYNASTIES 1070~767 B.C.

Rulers from LIBYA

Priest-kings in THEBES

MINOR RULERS

LATE PERIOD 767~525 B.C.

25TH DYNASTY

Rulers from NUBIA such as PIYE, SHABAKO, SHEBITKU, and TAHARQA

26TH DYNASTY

Pharaohs such as PSAMTIK I, NECHO II, AMASIS, and PSAMTIK II

Wouldn't all of these people be amazed if they knew they were ancient and that they've all been dead for thousands of years? I'm sure amazed. I have been all day! Hey! Who's that?
You are seeing Cleopatra, Queen of the Nile.
Most fortunate boy!
PERSIAN EMPIRE
PERSIAN PERIOD
525 ~ 332 B.C.
27TH, 28TH, 29TH, and 30TH DYNASTIES
332 B
CAMBYSES conquers EGYPT 525 B.C.
DARIUS I
XERXES
ARTAXERXES I
DARIUS II
AMYRTAEUS
HAKORIS
NECTANEBO I
DJEDHOR
NECTANEBO II
ARTAXERXES III
ARSES
DARIUS III
ALEXANDE the GREAT, 24-year-old King MACEDONIA, drives out the PERSIA

EMPIRE of
ALEXANDER the
GREAT

GREEK PERIOD

332~30 B.C. (PTOLEMAIC DYNASTY 323~30 B.C.)

MACEDONIAN KINGS
PHILIP   ALEXANDER
ARRHIDAEUS   IV

PTOLEMY I
(one of Alexander's
generals)
to PTOLEMY XI

CLEOPATRA
II
PTOLEMY
XII

QUEEN
BERENICE   PTOLEMY
IV   XIII

The legendary
CLEOPATRA VII tries –
and fails – to keep what was left
of EGYPT's power by
making alliances with
JULIUS CAESAR, then MARK ANTONY,
rulers of ROME, the most
powerful empire in her world.

PTOLEMY XV
(CAESARION)
son of
JULIUS CAESAR
and
CLEOPATRA

THE WELL·GROOMED EGYPTIAN

Hot sun and desert wind are hard on skin, so whether they were rich or poor, ancient Egyptians used lots of sweet-smelling ointments. To look good and avoid head lice, they often covered their shorn heads with intricate wigs. Men, women, and even children used ground-up plants and minerals to accent their eyes and lips.

Perfumed wax will melt and release sweet fragrance.

BRONZE MIRROR

Men and women outlined their eyes with KOHL (ground-up *galena*, a lead ore).

Containers for ointments, makeup, and face cream

RAZOR

WOOD or IVORY COMB

WALLS were whitewashed to reflect away the hot SUN.

PET MONKEY

Sipping lumpy, nutritious barley beer through a strainer-straw

For storage most people used BASKETS made of palm leaves, cane, or papyrus.

GRAIN was stored here.

Are the people wearing wigs? Oh, man—even the guys look like they're wearing makeup!

Very customary, dear.

After the fall of CLEOPATRA, EGYPTIANS were governed by ROMAN rulers. ROME'S grip did not weaken until

VENT
for cooling breezes

For privacy and to keep out dust, windows were high.

HEAD REST

OIL LAMP

BEE-HIVES

SPINNING
flax fibers into linen threads

WEAVING

WHAT'S FOR DINNER
Wheat or barley BREAD might be baked in a clay mold placed in the coals.

Flat bread, baked on a hot stone, might be rolled around lentils, egg, and/or vegetables.
FISH or FOWL was sometimes eaten, as was red meat on very seldom, special occasions.

MELON
FIGS
PLUMS
POMEGRANATE
HONEY CAKE
PALM FRUITS
GRAPES
DATES
BREAD
OLIVES
ONIONS
PEAS
LENTILS
CHICK PEAS
LEEK
CUCUMBER
RADISHES
EGGS
MILK and CHEESE
WINE
BEER
FISH

that empire broke apart in A.D. 395. By A.D. 642, EGYPT was again conquered - by the MUSLIMS of ARABIA.

THE WRITTEN WORD

These symbols of sounds and ideas stand for "King KHUFU."

Other people in ancient times made words with pictures, but the best known, hieroglyphs, were Egyptian. They were carved in stone or drawn with ink (soot plus water) and pens made from papyrus reeds. The papery scrolls were made from papyrus too. Business, government, Egypt's state religion—they couldn't run without documents. In a land and time where practically no one could read or write, scribes were very important.

Portable water bottle

Palette of dried ink

Whoa! This zip-zapping all over the place is making me dizzy. Hey, what is THIS? And who are THOSE guys? Where are those boys going? This place is almost TOO awesome!

This is the temple of Isis, and those are her priests. Those boys go to the temple's scribe school. It's very strict, but when they graduate, they'll be Egypt's communications experts.

See the shadows. It's the end of the day. The sun god is sinking and dying in the west. Will you go, Alexandria, or will you stay? That is your question. That is your test.
Zachary, hold out your hand and touch Khi's head—and my scarab here. When the last bit of sun disappears, you'll get zapped one more time—to the future.
What? With you, you mean?
No, I'm thinking I might stay here with the ancients. After all, I'm pretty ancient myself!
Huh? No, Auntie Allie! You've got to come back!
Quickly, Zach—the sun is setting! Good-bye, dear boy.
Good-bye, young man. Away with you!

Got turned around in this dang museum!
When you vanished, I knew that I . . . well . . .
Auntie Allie!
I'd miss you too, Auntie Allie.
If you guys are done whispering secrets, let's go eat. I'm hungry.

EGYPTIONARY

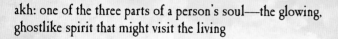

akh: one of the three parts of a person's soul—the glowing, ghostlike spirit that might visit the living

alabaster: a translucent stone, good for carving

amulet: a good-luck charm

Amun: The patron god of Thebes became known as Amun-Re when he was linked with the sun god.

ankh: symbol of life

Anubis: god of the dead and mummification, and lord of the necropolis (Greek for *cemetery*; "city of the dead")

ba: one of the three parts of a person's soul—the personality. Wall painters showed the *ba* as a human-headed bird.

Bastet: People came to Bubastis, in the Nile Delta (Lower Egypt), to worship this cat goddess of maternal protection.

Bes: half-dwarf, half-lion tambourine-playing god of the happy home and many children

Book of the Dead: spells and prayers written on scrolls and tombs meant to protect people in the underworld

canopic jars: special jars that held the body's embalmed liver, lungs, intestines, and stomach

cartouche: a ropelike ring of symbolic protection around the names of royal persons on monuments

cataract: river rapids. The ancient Nile River had six of them.

Delta: where the mouth of the Nile fans out. In ancient times it fanned into seven tributaries that flowed into the Mediterranean Sea.

dynasty: a line of kings and queens who are related to one another

ANKH

BA

CARTOUCHE

eye of Horus: In the myth the god Horus lost his eye in a fight, then got it back. This *wedjat* eye became a good-health amulet.

Geb: god of earth and plants; brother and husband of Nut, the goddess of the sky

Great Sphinx: The then 1,100-year-old man-headed lion of Giza was almost buried in sand around 1400 B.C., when, it is said, a young prince slept in its shadow. He had a dream: If he cleared the sand away, said the Sphinx, he would be king. So he did, and Thutmose IV became pharaoh.

Hathor: cow-horned mother goddess. Some scrolls speak of seven Hathors, who gave each Egyptian seven souls at birth.

hieroglyph: The word comes from Greek words for "sacred carving. Egyptians developed these symbols of objects, sounds, and ideas around 3000 B.C.

Horus: divine child of Isis and Osiris

Isis: Some old scrolls say the yearly flood of the Nile was caused by a teardrop from her eye. On the walls of her temples—found in ancient Greece and Rome, too—she's shown sailing in a moon boat across the sky.

ka: one of the three parts of a person's soul—the life force

lotus: a water lily. It symbolized Upper (southern) Egypt.

Maat: The feather that this goddess wore in her hair was the symbol of truth and justice.

mastaba: a slope-sided, bench-shaped Old Kingdom tomb made of mud bricks or stone

Middle Kingdom: an era, 2061–1668 B.C., in Egyptian history

natron: an antibacterial salt used for drying out a corpse as it was being mummified

SACRED
EYE of
HORUS

LOTUS

Nephthys: protector of women, and with her sister, Isis, represented life and death

New Kingdom: an era, 1560–1070 B.C., when Egypt was the greatest power in the ancient world. Some of Egypt's best-known monarchs, such as Hatshepsut, Tutankhamun, and Ramses II, reigned during the New Kingdom.

Nut: Every night this sky goddess swallowed up the sun god, Re, and gave birth to him every dawn.

obelisk: a tall, four-sided, pyramid-topped stone tower that stood for the sun's power. The Washington Monument is an obelisk.

OBELISK

ld Kingdom: an era, 2705–2213 B.C., in Egyptian history

siris: god of the underworld and eternal life. In the old
rth he was killed by his brother, Seth, god of chaos, but
s brought him back to life. The brother-sister marriage of
s and Osiris was mirrored in the ceremonial brother-sister
ions in Egypt's royal families.

pyrus: Fibers from this graceful water reed were
ed to make a kind of paper. Its flower stood for
wer (northern) Egypt.

araoh: The Egyptian word for "royal palace" came to
an the person who lived there. After the kingdom
s united, the pharaoh's two-part crown represented
per and Lower Egypt. The crown's carved cobra
od for the king's protection and doom for all
emies of Egypt.

ah: a creator god of craftsmen

(aka Ra): the sun god

setta stone: The three different languages
ved on this slab of stone discovered in Rosetta, Egypt, in
99 made it possible for modern people to decipher the writing of
ient Egypt.

cophagus: a coffin. Often more than one coffin (made of
ier-mâché, wood, or stone) nested together to contain the corpse.

The LIGHTHOUSE
OF
ALEXANDRIA

SPHINX

scarab: an amulet made to look like a dung beetle. It symbolized rebirth after death.

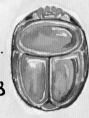

SCARAB

Seven Wonders of the Ancient World:
On ancient travelers' must-see list were
(1) the three largest pyramids at Giza in Egypt;
(2) the Hanging Gardens of Babylon, built around
600 B.C. near modern-day Baghdad, Iraq;
(3) the temple of the goddess Artemis, or Diana, built about
550 B.C. at Ephesus, on the western coast of Asia Minor
(modern-day Turkey);
(4) the gold-and-ivory statue of Zeus, king of the gods,
built about 435 B.C. at Olympia, Greece;
(5) the marble mausoleum (tomb) at Halicarnassus, the tomb
of a Persian ruler, built around 353 B.C. in southwestern Asia
Minor;
(6) a bronze statue of Helios, the sun god, called the
Colossus of Rhodes (an island in the Aegean Sea); and
(7) a 400-foot-tall lighthouse built around 280 B.C. on the
island of Pharos in the harbor of Alexandria.
Of all of these wonders, only the oldest, the pyramids, remain.

Shu: the old creator god who parted Nut, his starry
sky-goddess daughter, from his earth-god son, Geb

Sobek: crocodile god of fertility and water

Thoth: a moon god of wisdom, writing, and the scribes.
He was imagined with an ibis head or that of a baboon.

Valley of the Kings: the rocky burial ground of the pharaohs
for 500 years. It and the Valley of the Queens (for royal
wives and children) lay across the Nile River from the city
of Thebes.

vizier: the most powerful minister in the pharaoh's
government.

EGYPTOLOGY

Beyond Flint Knives and Copper Chisels

ANCIENT EGYPTIANS DEVISE TOOLS OF THE MIND: WAYS OF UNDERSTANDING, BUILDING, RECORDING, AND HEALING.

* With their observations of the sun and Sirius, the night's brightest star, they invented a 365-day solar calendar and divided each day into segments: twenty-four hours. Other ancient peoples, such as the Chinese, Hebrews, and Babylonians, based their calendars on the moon.
* Egyptians used their knowledge of arithmetic, astronomy, and engineering when they built the bases of pyramids almost perfectly square and lined up with the points of the compass.
* Ancient Egyptians invented the first national government as well as hieroglyphic: an imaginative, flexible written language.
* Egyptian doctors were greatly respected in the ancient world. Papyrus documents of ailments and cures were the first medical textbooks.

The basalt stone was found near Rosetta (Rashīd), EGYPT.

1822: FRENCH CODECRACKER SOLVES CENTURIES-OLD PUZZLE!

In 196 B.C. someone wrote a message on a black stone slab. In 1799 French soldiers found this "Rosetta stone." The message was written in Greek, an Egyptian script, and hieroglyphic, the picture language of ancient Egypt, which no one alive could read. For fourteen years Jean-François Champollion studied the letters and symbols. Finally in 1822 he cracked the code of hieroglyphic, a language of symbols for ideas and sounds.

Your next appointment? Let me check my calendar.

CLEOPATRA

NOVEMBER 26, 1922: BRITISH ARCHAEOLOGIST FINDS GOLDEN TREASURES IN TOMB OF "TUT," TEENAGE KING OF THE NILE! AMAZING DISCOVERY IGNITES WORLDWIDE INTEREST IN ANCIENT EGYPT. MYSTERIOUS DEATHS IGNITE RUMORS OF THE
MUMMY'S CURSE.

Tutankhamun slept in his golden coffins, surrounded by clothing, furniture, weapons, model boats, walking sticks, and all else he might need in the afterlife. Unlike those of other rulers of Egypt, his tomb was undisturbed—until Howard Carter found it. Light shone on the golden mask of the boy king for the first time in 3,200 years. Some of the people who were involved in the great discovery died in ways that seemed mysterious but have since been explained. Legends of cursed tombs have inspired countless books, movies, and nightmares.

To my nephew, the real, live Zachary

SIMON & SCHUSTER BOOKS FOR YOUNG READERS
An imprint of Simon & Schuster Children's Publishing Division
1230 Avenue of the Americas, New York, New York 10020
Copyright © 2004 by Cheryl Harness
SIMON & SCHUSTER BOOKS FOR YOUNG READERS is a trademark of Simon & Schuster, Inc.
Book design by Lucy Ruth Cummins
The text for this book is set in Mixagel IT and Caslon Antique.
The illustrations for this book are rendered in pen-and-ink and watercolor.
Manufactured in China
2 4 6 8 10 9 7 5 3 1
CIP data for this book is available from the Library of Congress.
0-689-83478-0

BIBLIOGRAPHY
Bonewitz, Ronald L. *Teach Yourself Hieroglyphics*. Chicago: Contemporary Books, 2001.
Casson, Lionel, and the editors of Time-Life Books. *Ancient Egypt*. New York: Time-Life Books, 1965.
Donoughue, Carol. *The Mystery of the Hieroglyphs*. New York: Oxford University Press, 1999.
Editors of Time-Life Books. *What Life Was Like on the Banks of the Nile*. Alexandria, VA: Time-Life Books, 1996.
Frank, John. *The Tomb of the Boy King*. New York: Farrar, Straus, and Giroux, 2001.
Green, John. *Life in Ancient Egypt*. New York: Dover Publications, 1989.
Gregory, Kristiana. *Cleopatra VII, Daughter of the Nile*. New York: Scholastic, 1999.
Hart, George. *Ancient Egypt*. New York: Dorling Kindersley, 1990.
Macaulay, David. *Pyramid*. New York: Houghton Mifflin, 1975.
Scott, Joseph, and Lenore Scott. *Hieroglyphs for Fun*. New York: Van Nostrand Reinhold, 1974.
Steedman, Scott. *Egyptian Town*. Danbury, CT: Franklin Watts, 1998.